Strangers in Your Mind

Also by Dimitri Chakhov,

Your Awesome Intellect: *How to Reboot the Right Side of Your Mind*

The Curious Occurrence of Life: *Which Scientific Discovery Proves God?*

Recharge Your Mission: *What Theory Is So Widely Accepted People Believe It's True*

If You Feel Lost: *What Important Condition of Your Life You Don't Know*

Strangers in Your Mind

How Emotions Change Your Spiritual Destiny

Dimitri Chakhov

DC books

ISBN: 978-1-989696-20-0

"Do not be anxious about your life."

(Matthew 6:25)

Table of Contents

1. My Worrying Mind 7
2. Deception 12
3. The Non-Self 18
4. The Venom of Anger 25
5. His Enemy Came and Sowed Weeds 30
6. You're What You Think 36
7. The Damaging Force 40
8. Stranger than Fiction 43
9. The Mysterious Event 49
10. The Deviation 52
11. Profit and Loss 57
Acknowledgements 62

1. My Worrying Mind

The Mind Game

I was in transition between bachelorhood and married life, which is a stressful time for most men. I wasn't handling the transition well. I felt that I was failing in my new role of husband and father.

"What's the matter?" I thought. I wasn't accustomed to feeling like a failure.

Soon, I realized the issue. I was suffering from repeated episodes of anxiety, which were getting increasingly stronger and lengthier.

"Anxiety?" I thought with disgust. "What the heck? How did I become such a sad sack?"

Was I overwhelmed by the weight of new responsibilities?

Was it something already broken inside of me?

I didn't know the answer. Either way, recognizing my own anxiety was the point when I started paying attention to my thoughts.

It was summer and we decided to get out of the city. We rented a cottage on a beautiful lake. The first evening, when my wife and our baby daughter were sleeping tired after a long day, I went outside.

Sitting on the porch, I looked at the dark waters of the lake.

"What is going on with me?" I thought.

I had no courage to tell my wife about the problem. I was supposed to be the force that would carry our young family through all of our obstacles and troubles. Instead, I was becoming the burden. I was afraid that my wife would notice my weakness. She'd already asked me (on a few occasions) what was wrong. I blamed tiredness. "Too much to do at work, you know."

Looking at the dark waters, I tried to analyze my thoughts. It became clear to me that I had gotten in the habit of worrying. I worried about many things every day—the well-being of my family, my job security, the health of our baby daughter, the possibility of a global economic meltdown, the deteriorating environment, and so on.

"Isn't it ordinary to worry about life?" I thought. "The future is unknown, which is why we worry more often than not."

Yet, my worries grew. Some days, I couldn't stop worrying; my thoughts wouldn't slow down. At night, I would have trouble falling asleep. Sometimes, my racing thoughts would keep me up until morning.

I was getting paranoid that my anxiety episodes were becoming a serious problem. I was getting anxious *about* my anxiety. I feared that this damaging force would change my personality and ruin my life. I felt as if the gate of my mind was made from some thin material; it was too shaky to keep out the invasive and persistent force of anxiety that was storming in.

I needed something to hold on to. I sat on the bench and drank herbal tea. I felt pathetic drinking herbal tea on a Friday night, but I had given up beer a week earlier. I decided that alcohol wouldn't help in my situation.

"It's a mind game," I thought as I looked at the sky. The wind picked up and dark night clouds moved in, covering the stars and moon.

"It's a mind game," I said quietly to myself. "It's a freaking mind game, and I'm losing it."

For some reason, the word *game* gave me relief. It's a game; anxiety is my opponent, and I must outplay it. I should be able to do that. Anxiety is a dark, hostile, and persistent force. But success in a mind game doesn't depend on brute force. I would need wit and wisdom to outsmart my opponent. But was I smart enough? Only time would tell.

Suddenly, I felt hope in my heart. It was a great feeling.

Hope

"The choice of words is important," I thought next morning.

Choosing the right words helps. If you say, "I'm sick," you imply that something is wrong with you. You're making yourself weak. If you say, "My mind is under assault," you're putting yourself into the shoes of a warrior. It's not your fault when a hostile force invades your mind. You do what you're supposed to do—you spot the danger and accept the challenge. You accept the necessity of the fight.

In the same way, hope is the opposite of worry. When you worry, you expect to lose. When you hope, you anticipate winning.

The next morning, I attempted to re-create the hopeful feeling, but it wasn't coming back. What had I done to trigger hope the night before? As I sat by the water, I had tried to think rationally and understand how anxiety works. The understanding made me hopeful.

"To be successful in dealing with anxiety," I thought, "I need a clear understanding of what is happening in my head."

Worries

Soon, I realized that there was something odd about worrying.

Typically, it requires a lot of effort to produce an original idea. But that isn't the casc with worries; they come effortlessly. Sometimes worries are forceful and intrusive. They intrude on our thoughts, and interrupt and halt creative thinking. Often, I find myself worrying even though I've intended to think about something else. Worries are easy to come, but hard to let go of.

That's not all. Besides the fact that anxiety is unpleasant, it can also be harmful. Sometimes, worries drag a soul into a state of depression. The alarming thing is that thoughts and feelings can cause such misery. Why would your own thinking try to ruin your life? It doesn't make sense. Why would your mind craft thoughts whose aim is devastation? Why do worries trap your mind in endless loops such that you can't stop being worried for days?

It seemed to me that worries were not like ordinary thoughts, so I tried to stay calm and think rationally about what anxiety really was.

"On the one hand," I thought, "there are real reasons to be concerned."

It was not as if I was just being silly and imagining all these things that worried me. The trend of outsourcing jobs was ongoing, global economic meltdowns came one after another, and the deterioration of the environment was very real.

On the other hand, *worrying* about these things wouldn't help resolving them.

I got intrigued by negative emotions. It was as if some weird mental beast was screwing with my mind. I wanted to get to the bottom of it.

2. Deception

Theory of Self-Deception

I spent a lot of time searching for ideas that could explain why I was getting anxious thoughts. In clinical psychology, there is a theory of self-deception in which a person acquires a bad habit, like a drug addiction, and then becomes afraid to admit it. As a result, he convinces himself that he's not addicted.[i] Such conviction is called self-deception.

Yet, self-deception doesn't harm the person; the drug addiction does. Self-deception is a passive state of mind when a person doesn't want or is afraid to deal with reality. A passive state of mind is not dangerous by itself. It is the external element—drugs or alcohol—that is dangerous.

It didn't seem to me that anxiety could be explained by self-deception alone. A mind is an intellectual rational element. It could get lazy and overlook or neglect the threat, but a mind has no reason to develop deceptive thoughts—i.e., worries—whose sole purpose is to harm.

"Self-deception happens," I thought, "when we fail to recognize an external danger, such as drugs or alcohol. Anxiety is the actual danger, and the failure to recognize it is self-deception."

The Danger Within

Anxiety is a danger you can't escape. You can't hide from it behind locked doors; you can't run from it by moving to a different country. It follows you wherever you go because it's the danger within.

How can you avoid it?

Well, anxiety is deceptive. I used to think that worries were beneficial because they warned me about potential dangers. But I soon recognized that worries were filling my heart with fear. Instead of being alarmed and alerted, I became fearful and depressed. It made me more vulnerable than I was before. In the end, anxiety achieved the opposite effect.

Throughout my life, I've learned a few things, and recognizing deceit is one of them. If I've been promised easy earnings but find myself losing money rather than profiting, I know that I've been deceived. Too bad that understanding often happens after the fact.

I looked at worries from the deception point of view.

The act of deception involves two parties: a fraudulent perpetrator and a naïve victim. The goal of deception is to transfer some value from the victim to the perpetrator. Such a transaction is usually done by misleading the victim.

To dupe the victim, a fake idea is employed. The fake scheme promises that the victim will gain great benefits for a small price.

Once the victim believes it, he becomes vulnerable and easy to manipulate. Eventually, the victim is convinced to transfer his value to the perpetrator.

Let's look at a lottery scam as an example. A lottery scam is a type of advance-fee fraud, which begins with an unexpected email explaining that you have won a large sum of money. The recipient of the message—the target—is told to contact a "claims agent" immediately. After contacting the agent, the target will be asked to pay a "processing fee" or a "transfer charge" so that the winnings can be distributed.[ii] After paying all fees and charges, the target never receives any lottery payment.

"Worries drop into my mind like scam emails into my inbox," I thought. I liked the metaphor. It was easy for me to deal with anxiety if I thought about worries as an external element.

"I shouldn't identify myself with worries," I thought. "They are my opponent."

The Intruder

The consulting start-up company I was working for as a software developer was struggling periodically to sustain the cash-flow. Every time the situation would get worse, rumors about potential lay-offs surfaced. I had a mortgage to pay and a young family to support, and I felt extremely vulnerable to such rumors.

How could I overcome anxiety in such uncertain circumstances?

I started thinking about anxiety as a con artist who was tirelessly trying to fool me. The idea was that a worry is an external perpetrator rather than the output of my own thinking.

The perpetrator wants to fool me, and for this purpose, he sends me deceitful messages. These messages take the shape of worry, and it pops up into my head just like the scam email. If I read it, recognize it as a scam, and delete it, then I am fine. Yet, if I accept it as a legitimate thought, my mind would be compromised.

For most of my life, I paid no attention to the mental events that were unfolding in my own head, and this lack of attention helped the intruder succeed in overtaking me. I was letting my mind get worried because I didn't recognize a worry as a hostile and deceitful force. As a result, I worried about potential events like a lay-off (which would never actually materialize).

All the while, I overlooked the *real* dangerous element: the mental intruder that we call anxiety.

Fighting Back

At some point, I began to believe that I was indeed dealing with an external hostile force that was trying to penetrate and mess with my mind.

It's one thing when you think that you're dealing with your own weaknesses; by doing so, you're more likely to accept them as your own personal traits. But it's different when you realize that you're the target of a deceptive scheme. Then you don't want to lose, because it's shame to be deceived by the same trick so many times.

If I gave into anxiety, I could lose all the good things that had finally started happening to me— the love for my daughter and wife. Anxiety made me unreliable.

The realization that an external force was trying to ruin me in the best time of my life made me furious. It made me eager to fight back.

"A nation suffers when it's occupied by a foreign force," I wrote in my notes. "A defeated nation has no reason to be optimistic in its outlook for the future, because an occupying force exploits both land and people. The same happens to a mind occupied by a foreign force. It has no future until it regains its independence. I must rebel against occupying force, which is my anxiety. I must rebel!"

I tried to resist all the anxious thoughts creeping into my mind day and night. I imagined myself as a powerful man standing in a room with a sharp, shiny sword in his hands. Anxious thoughts were rats that tried to get into the room, storming through windows and doors. Any time an anxious thought appeared in my mind, I would slash it with the sword. I aimed to kill the rats so they would never come back.

At night, sitting beside our daughter's crib, I repeated in my mind again and again that I could not lose this battle. Looking at her beautiful sleeping face, I thought, "I should fight back until I win. I can't accept defeat. I can't let my soul become broken."

The Irony of Anxiety

Maybe you often worry that your life could be ruined by an accident, sickness, crime, or loss of income. Any of these unfortunate events could suddenly affect you, and you can't control it. And yet, you can't add security to your life by being anxious.

Thankfully, you have the ability to control your mind. Anxiety uses your lack of control over external events as a reason to intrude in your thoughts. When you become anxious, you don't gain control over outside events; rather, you temporarily lose control over your own mind.

The irony is that when you intensively worry about potential loss, you already have suffered a mental defeat.

"Isn't it strange?" I thought. "My own thoughts cause chaos in my head. My whole life can be easily wasted in endless loops of anxious thoughts."

I resolved myself to find out more.

3. The Non-Self

Arrogance

It was a routine departmental meeting. Our manager Matt was forming a team for a new project, and I was eager to get included. I'd finished my last project a week ago and had been relatively free since then. The lack of projects on my desk always made me anxious. In addition, Matt said that the new project could require potential travel to France to meet a client. Who doesn't want to go on a business trip to France?

"And Rick will do the database development," Matt said, pointing at my co-worker.

The team was formed, but I had wanted the role of the database developer for myself.

"Matt," I said, "what about me? I'm not busy right now. I have all the qualifications."

"I know, Dimitri," he said, "but we already have enough people. I'll give you Brad's projects to finish."

Brad had quit a few days ago. Everybody knew that all his projects were a mess.

"Thank you for entrusting me with this challenging task," I said.

"You can do it, Dimitri," Rick said sarcastically. "We believe in you."

I didn't find his sarcasm appropriate. I didn't doubt that I could do it. I just didn't want to do it, because it's a bummer finishing somebody else's project. You don't know what parts of code work properly, so you have to test everything. I doubted that Brad left any comments in his code.

I looked at Rick's smiling face and registered nasty thoughts popping up in my mind. According to these notions, Rick was a stupid, unskilled, and unreliable individual.

"Look at him, he is such a miserable, worthless man," I thought.

Rick was an arrogant fellow and, I guess for this reason, I felt especially bitter. If Matt had chosen somebody else, I wouldn't have been so upset. But Matt picked arrogant Rick over me, and this bothered me.

Later that night during my meditation hour, the same thoughts were still popping up in my head. I wasn't able to calm my mind that evening.

Character

A person's character is a collection of his distinctive mental and moral qualities. Moral qualities are shaped by mental efforts. The lack of effort disfigures the character. For example, my inability to keep anxiety at bay had harmed my character.

The benefit of having a decent character is obvious. You like to surround yourself with quality things. They make life easier and more enjoyable. Likewise, surrounding the inner-self with high quality thoughts should improve the quality of your life.

A weak character is usually associated with harboring annoying and persistent habits, and being constantly worried is one of them. The need to judge and criticize friends, relatives, coworkers, and neighbors is another bad habit.

Taking interest in somebody else's flawed character seems like an awful waste of time. Why, then, was I so invested in Rick? Why did it give me such pleasure to think bad about him? Was I as arrogant as he was?

The Irony of Arrogance

Why should you seek improvement of your character? Having a well-rounded, stable character makes your life more pleasant.

The improvement of the character happens when you increase the quality of thinking. The process starts with identifying your own flaws. For example, I had a habit of worrying, and then I realized that it was a harmful habit. Now, I deal with it and I keep working on myself.

Arrogance is the belief that you're better, smarter, or more important than others. Arrogance often pops up in your thoughts when your significance isn't recognized by other people.

At first glance, it appears that arrogance offers some kind of comfort. It seems like a justified reaction to think about self-importance when others underappreciate you. If people don't recognize you as an important person, you won't recognize them in retaliation.

It is the moment when the "theft" happens. This is because your state of mind affects only *you*; you don't actually retaliate against other people when you become arrogant. You only retaliate against yourself because you're letting the state of your mind be changed for the worse.

You're becoming better as you improve your character. When you seek improvement, you observe the behavior of other people and take note of their good traits. Then you try to develop similar qualities.

On the contrary, arrogance prevents you from seeing the good in others and the faults in yourself. The irony is that arrogance comes with the belief that you're better than others. Yet, as soon as you accept an arrogant notion, you become a shallower person.

The Virus of Emotions

It surely feels as if all your thoughts and emotions originate in your mind. But why would your own thoughts try to corrupt you? It doesn't make sense. Why would your own thoughts persistently try to change the state of your mind for the worse?

I was desperate to understand how it happens, and then I thought about viruses.

Biological viruses are found wherever there is life. Viruses can infect all types of life forms, from animals and plants to bacteria and single-celled microorganisms.

All life on earth is under constant pressure from viruses.[iii] If the immune system of a living organism becomes compromised, sooner or later the organism will become infected with a virus. As a result, many human diseases are caused by viral infections.

A biological virus is a small infectious agent. The name "virus" is from a Latin word meaning "slimy liquid" or "poison." Viruses are not free-living organisms; they are parasites. They depend on the host cell for almost all of their life-sustaining functions. They even can't reproduce without a host cell.

The true infectious part of any virus is its DNA. The goal of the virus is to penetrate a living cell and to trick it into reproducing the virus' DNA instead of the cell's own DNA.[iv]

"Would be it far-fetched," I thought, "to consider negative emotions as similar to biological viruses?"

Like viruses, negative emotions are not free-living beings. They're parasites, because they too need a host-mind to flourish. Like viruses, they try to penetrate the host-mind and fool it into reproducing the specific emotion instead of its own thinking. Just as a biological virus replaces a cell's DNA with its own, a mental virus replaces the genuine thoughts of the mind with negative emotions. Both biological viruses and negative emotions are harmful to the host organism (or host mind, in this case).

Biological viruses are energy parasites; they derive energy from the host cell. Similarly, negative emotions drain energy from your mind.

The Immune System

The immune system protects the physical body from harmful viruses and bacteria. To accomplish this task, the immune system must recognize and neutralize harmful parasites that enter the body.

For this protection to be effective, the immune system must differentiate between its own cells and intruders.[v] The immune system wouldn't work if it were not able to differentiate between "self" and "non-self" cells.

Like viruses, negative emotions are also opportunistic. They cannot sustain themselves and they seek opportunities to infiltrate a weakened mind, just as biological viruses take the opportunity to infiltrate a weakened immune system. When you're in a critical situation, your mind gets under pressure and parasitic mental notions break-in, corrupting your thoughts.

If you're unable to differentiate between "self" and "non-self" notions, then you easily accept "non-self" anxiety or arrogance as your own thoughts. It could make you mentally sick. Your spiritual immune system could become compromised: it's no longer able to recognize and neutralize harmful parasitic emotions.

And so the negativity within you begins to grow.

Doubts

Yet, I struggled to believe my own conclusion.

"Are all my worries completely external to me?" I thought.

It hardly could be true. No doubt, I often worry on my own accord. How then was I supposed to differentiate between my own thoughts and thoughts caused by a mental virus, between "self" and "non-self" emotions?

I couldn't answer this question. Maybe there was no clear line. Maybe I needed to develop this skill by paying continuous attention to all thoughts going on in my head.

"When you're running fast," I wrote in my notebook one of those days, "you can't stop immediately; you need to make a few steps to reduce the speed gradually. Similarly, the mind has inertia too. If you think deeply, you can't stop immediately; you need to make an effort to calm your thoughts. With effort, you can stop your own thinking. When you feel powerless to stop repetitive notions like fear, greed, arrogance, or anxiety, then they are the work of a mental virus."

4. The Venom of Anger

Road Rage

I'd always been sure that I was a nice guy, nearly perfect in most ways. Then I started noticing cracks in my character. First, I was devastated to realize that I was subject to reoccurring episodes of anxiety. Next, I discovered that I was no stranger to arrogance. What else was hidden in the depths of my soul?

Well, for one, I would get angry easily.

For example, I would get mad whenever somebody cut me off on the highway. Don't you hate these people who drive recklessly and disrespectfully to others? So, what would happen next? I would become angry and mutter an obscenity. Often, I would want to do something bad to that person, teach him a lesson somehow. But usually, I would do nothing; I'd just get angry.

Almost certainly, that person who cut me off was already full of anger or arrogance. Maybe he was angry for some specific reason; maybe he is always this way. Anger and arrogance made him behave irrationally and dangerously on the road.

What can we say about me? Before the encounter, I was a peaceful, lawful, minding-my-own-business type of citizen. In other words, I was a nice fellow. My angry reaction was spontaneous, and it seemed reasonable to get angry with that disrespectful person.

But let's leave that soul alone; he drove away and took his troubles with him. Let's look at what happens to the nice fellow. I become not so nice. For a second, I become exactly like him—angry and arrogant. It's a little bit strange.

His bad driving was the perfect example of why it's bad to be angry, because you become irrational and stupid and ignore those around you. Yet, I let myself become the same. Why? Because I wanted to retaliate, get even. I wanted to punish the wrongdoer. I let myself get angry.

The Venomous Drink

Let's say that anger is a venomous drink. When someone drinks it, he becomes irrational and loses control over his thoughts. The venom chokes everything good in his soul and pushes him to do bad things: to insult, assault, bring physical or psychological harm to others.

On the highway, I encountered a person who hurt my feelings because he was drunk with this venom. Would it make sense for me to grab a glass with the same venom and drink it immediately? Whom am I punishing?

Yet, I found that it's hard to resist anger. Anger quickly gives you reasons to be irritated. As lightning illuminates the dark night sky, anger fills your mind with an urgency to respond.

It builds into an overpowering feeling that you can't tolerate something or somebody anymore. Your mind suddenly gets in such a state that you don't see any other option but to become angry.

When I'm on the highway—and I commute every day—it seems to me that all the other drivers are in my way. I get enraged with those who drive too slowly, blocking the lane and not letting me pass. I'm also furious with those who drive too fast, because they create dangerous situations. The worse thing is, I can't stop being angry in spite of my understanding of anger's deceitful nature.

During my meditation hours, I clearly see that when I'm angry, I lose control over my mind. I recognize the need to resist anger. Yet, as I drive to work the next morning, if somebody in front of me is not driving fast enough and we are in the fast lane, I can't help but become angry.

Irony of Anger

Often, it seems that you are justified to get enraged. You get angry at injustice, discrimination, and oppression. Fury arises in your heart when you're hurt or mistreated by others, when you're a victim of an insult or an assault. It seems like anger fuels your desire to make the world a better place.

But you can't make the world a better place by becoming bitter and bad-tempered. When you are angry, you become worse than you were a moment before. Accordingly, the world becomes worse, because now it has fewer good people living in it.

Anger is deceitful because it makes you to do the same bad things that triggered your fury in the first place. Often, anger arises as a response to mistreatment, but once you become angry, you tend to mistreat other people. Anger isn't about eliminating injustice or violence, or getting rid of discrimination and abuse. Quite the opposite, it's about *enforcing* these things.

The Real Problem

My road rage would be amusing nonsense if it were all my troubles. The real problem was that I would get angry with my lovely baby daughter when she disobeyed me. I was getting angry as fast as a dry forest catching fire and I screamed at her. Then the next minute, I would sit on the floor beside her, ashamed, confused, and desperate.

"How did I lose my cool again?" I couldn't stop asking myself this as I watched her cry, and I felt guilt trickle down my spine.

There were times I would get angry with my wife when she didn't act the way I wanted her to act. I didn't scream at her because I knew that retaliation would follow. Yet, I felt that someday, I could lose it and release the fury of my thoughts on her, too.

Be a Wise King

To mobilize my inner powers for resistance, I personified anger. Anger was a ruthless thief that wanted to corrupt my mind. My task was to resist.

I imagined that my head was a small spiritual domain, a spiritual kingdom if you will. The 'I'—the spirit—is the king. The king's job is to rule the kingdom. The kingdom is small and only has a few inhabitants. These inhabitants were my good emotions: my love for my family and my hopes for a good future.

Since the king was slacking for a long time, the kingdom fell into a state of misery and distress. Now, the king is back. Yet, upon his return, he finds that the throne has been overrun by thieves.

The king is standing in the central plaza, and he sees that true inhabitants of the kingdom (love and hope) are suppressed and hiding in the dark, cold basements. The streets are full of flourishing thieves—anxiety, arrogance, jealousy, fear, greed, and anger.

What is the king going to do? Will he accept defeat? Then he won't be a king any longer. He will be a slave in his own kingdom. What a miserable destiny that is!

"Be a king," I would often say to myself. "Be a wise king and don't surrender your small but intricate and beautiful kingdom—your soul—to thieves."

5. His Enemy Came and Sowed Weeds

Dangerous Things

That fall, during the late hours, when the rest of my family was already sleeping, I used to seclude myself in my home office and read the Gospel.

In the beginning, I felt strange reading about things like the Heavenly Father and the heavenly kingdom. But I became captivated by Jesus' preaching and continued reading.

I had problems with my emotions, so I was looking for a practical advice in the Gospel.

Jesus often calls God the Heavenly Father.

"That's interesting," I thought.

As a father, I want my children to grow up smart. Most likely, the Heavenly Father doesn't want his children to grow up stupid, either.

I also want my daughter to be safe and healthy. For this reason, I'm repeatedly telling her about dangers appropriate to her age.

Right now, she is small, so I make it clear that she absolutely cannot insert anything into electrical outlets. When she grows up, I'll warn her about the dangerous nature of drugs.

Are there any spiritual dangers? If yes, then the Heavenly Father should warn us about them. I began examining Gospels from this point of view and was stunned. I found the verse where Jesus advises against anxiety!

> *"Therefore, I tell you, do not be anxious about your life, what you will eat or what you will drink, nor about your body, what you will put on." (Matthew 6:25)*

Over the course of raising my daughter, I learned that when prohibiting something, I should forbid only truly dangerous things. Otherwise, my commands would eventually lose their credibility.

Jesus advises avoiding anxiety. It means that worrying is a truly dangerous thing. Otherwise, Jesus wouldn't advise against it.

The Parable

Why are emotions so dangerous that Jesus speaks about them specifically? My own struggle with anxiety made me very curious. I wanted to understand the nature of emotions.

I read all four Gospels a few times, but I couldn't find explanations why anxiety is harmful. Slightly disappointed, I began studying Jesus' parables. Maybe Jesus explains emotions in a metaphorical form.

Then I came across the Parable of the Weeds. I had read it before but it hadn't attracted my attention. This time, I got intrigued by the parable.

Here it is,

Jesus told them another parable: "The kingdom of heaven is like a man who sowed good seed in his field. But while everyone was sleeping, his enemy came and sowed weeds among the wheat, and went away. When the wheat sprouted and formed heads, then the weeds also appeared.

"The owner's servants came to him and said, 'Sir, didn't you sow good seed in your field? Where then did the weeds come from?'

"'An enemy did this,' he replied.

"The servants asked him, 'Do you want us to go and pull them up?'

"'No,' he answered, 'because while you are pulling the weeds, you may uproot the wheat with them. Let both grow together until the harvest. At that time, I will tell the harvesters: First collect the weeds and tie them in bundles to be burned; then gather the wheat and bring it into my barn.'" (Matthew 13:24-30 NIV)

Conflict

"What does Jesus tell us here?" I thought.

The spiritual realm is no stranger to conflict and offence. While one force does good things, another force undermines the efforts of the good force. It sounds like a busy place.

Let's say that the owner of the field stands for the Heavenly Father. He is opposed by a hostile power.

This dark force is called "his enemy," and we sense that the enemy has a malicious nature. He comes under cover of the night and good deeds don't require the cover of darkness.

What else can we say about the enemy? He is not a fair competitor, and his actions are destructive. He hatched a harmful plan, and when everyone was sleeping, he secretly put his plan into action. He sowed the weeds.

The Mind-Field

"A man sowed good seed in his field."

What does the field stand for? When explaining the parable, Jesus says, "*The field is the world*" (Matthew 13:38). The Greek word *κόσμος (kosmos),* which is translated into English as "world," has a few meanings. Among others, it could mean

- Harmonious arrangement or order
- Universe
- Any collection of elements of any sort[vi]

Later, the term "field" was used in physics to describe electromagnetic waves produced by electrically charged objects. An electromagnetic field is a physical quantity that has a value for each point in space and time.[vii] A field affects the behavior of charged objects in its vicinity.

It could be that Jesus' vision is similar. Jesus sees the totality of humankind as a mentally charged field. Each spot on the field represents an individual human soul.

Good Seed

More likely, good seed stands for good teaching, because the previous parable of the Sower (Matthew 13:3-9) uses the image of seed in this meaning.

A human soul is the source of the wild, untapped mental energy. The Heavenly Father tries to cultivate our souls through teaching. Jesus describes the state of things in a short phrase,

> *"The kingdom of heaven is like a man who sowed good seed in his field."*

Wheat grows from seed. Similarly, morality and spiritual inspiration in our hearts must come from some source. According to the parable, the words of Jesus' preaching are such a source. When the word about the heavenly kingdom falls into your ears, it might encourage you to produce spiritual and moral efforts.

When seeds sprout, they become plants. This is the metaphor for the virtues of a human soul. Having hope improves your thinking. You try to govern your thoughts; you seek to fill your heart with courage, justice, love, hope, honesty, and loyalty. As a result, the virtues of your soul grow the way the wheat grows.

The grain ripens and the harvest time gets close. As life progresses, your moral efforts grow into permanent qualities of your soul.

Intrigue

The parable portrays the Heavenly Father as the supreme good being. He is good because He acts for the benefit of others. We feel that He is of a gentle nature. He doesn't rush into action to uproot weeds.

"It could mean," I thought, "that He avoids imposing his will on anybody. He respects humans' independent thinking and doesn't put pressure on our thoughts."

The good teaching should invoke good thoughts in your mind and inspire your soul to seek strength and growth.

Jesus adds intrigue to the parable by introducing the opposing force. The enemy doesn't like the idea of human moral growth. He wants to reverse the process. For this purpose, he sows the weeds.

The weeds must be some kind of an invasive and corruptive force that is designed to choke your good intentions. What then do the weeds stand for?

6. You're What You Think

The Choice

You are what you think.

You become good when you embrace good thinking habits. For example, from a moral point of view, it's good to be honest. The problem is that in real-life situations, your honesty often puts you at a disadvantage. To keep your souls honest, occasionally you must suffer losses, financial and otherwise. As such, you're regularly finding yourself struggling to make the right choice.

To make things more complicated, the Parable of the Weeds speaks about future consequences. At the final judgment, the souls with evil thoughts will be treated as weeds and burned. The souls with good thoughts will be viewed as the wheat and kept. Future consequences supposedly should reward good honest souls.

So, what should you do now? Should you be honest no matter what, even if it means you will suffer financial losses and other disadvantages? Or should you ignore the possibility of future spiritual consequences?

Clearly, the choice isn't easy. It would be a pity to miss the chance of having eternal life, but how can you be sure that it will truly happen? To be honest, you don't know.

The Evaluation

The parable of the Weeds speaks about the final judgment, and such an idea can't be exceedingly popular.

Most people don't like to go through tests, evaluations, or exams. You hate to be judged. Yet, you should look at the issue from the Heavenly Father's point of view. He has an estate—the heavenly kingdom—and he graciously agreed to share this estate with your soul.

The concept of evaluation is widely used in many aspects of life. School exams are a good example. Quality control at the end of a manufacturing process is another. In some places in North America, to rent an apartment you have to present references. References are used to evaluate your personality, because nobody likes to get stuck with bad tenants.

Presumably, your soul will live in the kingdom forever. If you look at things from this point, you see why the Heavenly Father can't welcome everyone. Otherwise, the tranquility of life in the kingdom would be spoiled very soon.

To prevent trouble, the Heavenly Father needs to evaluate his future tenants. The final judgment could be seen as such an event.

The Decision-Making Effort

Who would decide the eternal destiny of your soul? Would be it God, his angels, or maybe you? It seems that the Parable of the Weeds tells us that God's angels make this crucial decision. But how can we be certain?

Let's consider this. It seems that the destiny of a man who has committed a crime is decided in court.

It seems that the destiny of a man who has committed a crime is decided in court. However, it is his decision to break the law that shapes his life and destiny. He knew the possible consequences, but he decided to pursue his criminal intentions anyway. We can't fault the court for the man's broken life. It was the man's own decision that landed him behind the bars (assuming that the laws, the investigation, and the court procedures are not corrupt).

Similarly, you can't fault the angels if your soul ends up in the wrong bundle. They just evaluate what you have grown in your soul. Is it love or hate, hope or anxiety, courage or fears, faith or disbelief? Is it wheat or weeds?

You have your whole life to live—and it is *your* decisions on how you spend your time and for what purpose you engage your intellect. It is your decision what type of ideas and desires to cherish in your mind.

Signs of Upcoming Troubles

To spiritually unfulfilled people, Jesus delivers the good news. Human life isn't a freak accident in the middle of a vast and insensible space.

Jesus tells you that human life on earth is only a phase of a much greater spiritual process. It gives you strong motivation to overcome your struggles and suffering and keep your mind focused on good things.

The parable draws a rather dynamic image of reality. A farmer's field, which could be associated with hard-but-peaceful labor, is used as the main image. But peace doesn't last long. As the parable progresses, we learn about the opposing power that sets the conflict off. The owner of the field identifies the other acting power as the enemy. There might be some previous history of rivalry between them. The enemy invades the owner's field and inflicts damage by sowing weeds.

The owner displays calm and confidence. He decides to avoid direct confrontation—at least for now. Yet, we understand that the pristine quietness of the field is spoiled. The evil seeds were sown. They are growing. They are a sure sign of upcoming troubles.

7. The Damaging Force

Inhuman Practice

I grew up in a secular family and the Gospel ideas were novel to me.

Until then, I had been convinced that my life, deeds, and thoughts were my private business. According to Jesus' parable of the Weeds, however, it was my private business only until the end of time. When time is up, a soul leaves the body, enters into the open, and becomes a subject to evaluation.

On the one hand, it is certainly good news. The death of the body is not the end of human personal existence.

On the other hand, some Jesus' words made my skin crawl.

When explaining the Parable of the Weeds to his disciples, Jesus said,

> *"They will throw them into the blazing furnace, where there will be weeping and gnashing of teeth." (Matthew 13:42 NIV)*

You can sense from Jesus' description that hell is a brutal and inhumane place. You also can sense some disconnect here.

We are sinners by God's standard, but even we stopped punishing our criminals by torture. We don't burn them alive anymore; we lock them in cells. Why would loving, intelligent God allow such a barbaric and brutal practice?

This question causes many people to dismiss religion completely.

I felt myself cornered.

"The final judgment could be seen as an unfair event," I thought. "God inflicts severe penalties on us as retribution for the smallest offenses. It also seems that God's punishment significantly outdoes our faults."

A Damaging Force

Then I got this idea.

We see God as the force that brings eternal suffering on our souls. What if this is a wrong understanding.

I read the parable again.

"My soul is a tiny lot in the global mental field," I thought.

Two types of seeds good and evil have been sown into the field. If you carefully observe your mind, you notice three types of thoughts: neutral, good, and wicked. The parable concentrates on the last two types. Wheat stands for good thoughts, and weeds for the wicked.

If you neglect your mental lot, weeds will pollute it and choke the wheat. This is the moment when damage to your soul is done.

This damage happens now, not at the final judgment event. Avoiding damage is simple but not easy; you need to avoid wicked thoughts and appreciate the good ones.

Let's consider the following example. To cross a residential street, you must follow a few simple rules or you could be hit by a car. In such an event, the consequences are always worse than the mistake. A small error—you forgot to look to your right—could result in bruises, pain, broken bones, or concussion.

It is not the magnitude of your mistake, but the force of the moving car that causes damage. This is why you don't ignore cars when crossing the street. Does the parable convey a similar idea? Your small spiritual mistakes could lead to dreadful consequences. Yet, the mistakes don't damage you; they make you vulnerable to hostile spiritual forces. These forces cause the damage.

"The intent of Jesus' preaching is to help us," I thought.

The spiritual realm is a dangerous place. To navigate your ways successfully, you need to understand how it works and avoid collision with dangerous forces.

The weeds stand for the dangerous spiritual force.

8. Stranger than Fiction

Secular views on reality are bottom-up. According to these views, complex objects of reality are rising by the piecing together simpler elements. The origin of things tells us about their end. All complex elements will be eventually dissolved into elementary particles. Life ends with the death of a body. There is nothing above you. There is no God. Nobody is concerned with your life and death, and nobody would save your soul.

Religious views are top-down. According to religion, all elements of reality are created by a supreme intellectual force.

Jesus teaches the top-down view and he promises life after death. Yet, there are a few complications on your way to eternal life.

Free Will

The Weeds parable specifies two supreme powers.

The Heavenly Father is a supreme intelligent living being. He respects the independence of human intellect and doesn't impose His will on you. He embraces the freedom of choice, but such a liberal attitude causes some temporary difficulties.

We also learn that there is the enemy of the Heavenly Father, the devil. The difference between God and the devil shows in their position toward humankind.

God's influence on your decision-making process is minimal. He relies on your senses to follow a good teaching. God trusts your ability to come to the right decisions. Sometimes it seems that He trusts you too much.

We don't know the motivation of the devil, but his actions are suspicious. He doesn't rely on the freedom of choice and secretly plots to influence human minds. He wants to make sure that every soul ends up under his authority. It is a sign of bad intentions.

The Proxy War

The Heavenly Father doesn't rush into action to uproot weeds. He says, "*Let both grow together until the harvest.*" Before this decision, the moral state of the universe was regulated solely by two superpowers.

After that decision, a new force—humankind—gets drawn in the conflict. As it often happens, the major powers choose to fight a proxy war. The peaceful farmer's field becomes a battlefield. The front line of the moral conflict between good and evil is drawn through the human soul.

Reality is much stranger than we can ever imagine, because it was created by the superior intellect.

The Price of Freedom

Often, Jesus arrives at intense conclusions:

> *"Whoever says, 'You fool!' shall be liable to the hell of fire." (Matthew 5:22)*

Saying to somebody, "You fool!" isn't a horrific crime that warrants being burned alive in the hell of fire. We feel that this heavenly punishment grossly outweighs the actual harm of the offense. Our statement that God is good crumbles at this point.

What is the point of you having freedom if you could be burned alive for one wrong word?

Yet, before jumping to conclusions, let's consider this. God gifted you with intellect: maybe He expects you to use it intensely. Maybe Jesus uses strong words like 'the hell of fire', because he tries to wake up your sleeping mind. If calling somebody a fool causes such severe and lasting consequences, why don't you stop doing it?

We love to notice the shortcomings of others, even of God. Jesus advises to deal with our own flaws first.

The Malicious Attack

Negative emotions wait for opportunistic moments to sprout into action. A biological virus infects living organisms with weakened immune systems. Similarly, deceitful emotions attack the mind of an already stressed and unbalanced individual.

Anxiety immediately pops up in uncertain and potentially dangerous situations.

Arrogance arises when your self-esteem has been hurt.

Anger overwhelms your feelings if you've been insulted.

At its first appearance, a negative emotion tries to represent itself as a useful thought. A worry could be perceived as an early warning sign of danger, arrogance as inspiration to be better, and anger as a powerful desire for justice. They try to trick you just as the con artists try to trick you with scam emails. Thieves want your money. Emotions want your soul.

Emotions could be mistaken with native, genuine thoughts. The ability to distinguish between "self" and "non-self" notions is the sign of a mature soul.

The same basic programming technique, a loop, is used to conduct a mental attack. In programming, a loop is a repeated sequence of instructions while certain conditions are true.

Mental intruders use a similar technique. Anxiety repeatedly creates worrisome thoughts while you are in an uncertain situation. Anger repeatedly creates a fury in your heart while you're being unfairly treated. A loop is the perfect vehicle to deliver a malicious attack. With mechanical persistence, a fraudulent emotion pops up in your mind until you give in.

The Symptoms

> *"You have heard that it was said to the people long ago, 'You shall not murder, and anyone who murders will be subject to judgment.' But I tell you that anyone who is angry with a brother or sister will be subject to judgment." (Matthew 5:21-22 NIV)*

The old understanding of sin was associated with harmful actions like murder, stealing, and adultery. So why then did Jesus say that there is no big difference between a murderer and an angry person?

A murderer inflicts much more harm to other people than an angry person does. So why then are both subject to the same judgment? From our point of view, it seems like an unfair arrangement.

If you don't see emotions as mental parasites, they will eventually corrupt your mind. Emotions alter your thoughts, and then your emotional thoughts alter your behavior. Emotions make you act irrationally. The altered behavior (for example, saying, "You fool!") is a sign of an infection. Altered thoughts are the symptom.

Killing someone and calling somebody a fool are signs of the same spiritual problem. The symptoms could be severe or mild, but the problem is the same. The corrupted soul produces weeds rather than wheat.

Crossing to the Other Side

All my interpretations were based on the assumption that emotions are not genuine elements of our thinking. They are "non-self" notions that invade our minds. However, I couldn't prove it.

"What if am I wrong?" I doubted.

Later, I realized that there is no need for proofs. I don't need to convince anyone but myself. Everyone can observe their own emotions and come to their own ideas.

So what is my personal conclusion?

"Negative emotions cause harm to my mind and life," I thought.

The organisms own cells are not harmful to the body. Similarly, genuine thoughts shouldn't be harmful to the mind. It means that negative emotions are "non-self" mental elements.

Often, Jesus' teaching is perceived as restrictive. Are parents restrictive when they make sure that their child remembers the rules of crossing the street? The street is a dangerous place to play or walk because of the damaging force of moving cars. For this reason, you follow the rules when crossing a street.

Jesus has no intention to restrict your freedom for doing good things. He has no plans to diminish your desire to acquire the full spiritual strength of your character. But he advises you about spiritual dangers. He does it because he would like to see you cross to the other side.

Sometimes it seems that Jesus implies that God will punish you for ignoring his commands. It's a misunderstanding. Dangerous forces, when ignored, inflict damage. The Heavenly Father isn't a dangerous force; negative emotions are.

9. The Mysterious Event

"When the unclean spirit has gone out of a person, it passes through waterless places seeking rest, but finds none." (Matthew 12:43)

The Lot

During meditation hours, I'd learned how to calm my mind. It was a great joy to be in control of my thoughts.

"My mind is a ship," I wrote in my notes. "I need to master the skill how to navigate it in in the direction I want to go. I can't afford to let it drifting in the direction the wind of emotions blows."

The Wheat and Weeds parable made a significant impact on my worldview. I began seeing many things differently. I carefully investigated any spontaneous thoughts. I tried to cultivate good thinking habits.

Soil of the field is the source of inorganic nutrients for plants. Similarly, a mind is the source of mental energy, which let virtues of our soul to grow. If you neglect a piece of land, weeds would overgrow planted crops. Similarly, if you neglect the mind, negative emotions would push out good thoughts.

I tirelessly tried spotting and uprooting weeds from my thinking.

"I own this small mental lot, my mind and soul. I must put it in good use," I wrote in my notes.

I worked hard at my lot trying to change my arrogant-angry-worrying soul. I tried to plant good seeds: Hope instead of anxiety, love instead of anger and respect instead of arrogance.

The Unclean Spirit

I used to meditate every day. One day in the course of meditation, I noticed a strange thing.

I was concentrating my attention at an imaginable point in front of me. I tried keeping the mind continuously focused at this point. It was a new mental exercise. After a few minutes of concentration, I suddenly felt that the inner tension in my mind started to grow. At some point, I lost concentration.

"No problem," I thought. "Let's try one more time."

Then a strange thing happened. No matter how hard I tried, l would lose the concentration every time. It was as if I were holding a gate of the mind closed but some force on the other side of the gates pushed the gate wide open.

I was overwhelmed by that force every time I tried. Every time, I would try holding my focus at the imaginable point as long as possible. Every time, a mental wave would rise and pass through my mind breaking my concentration.

At first, I didn't give much significance to it. Then I was shocked.

"This is it," I thought. "It's an unclean spirit inside of my mind. When I'm entirely focused, I gain full control over my mind. This effort chokes the unclean spirit and cuts it from the energy source. It's the same like preventing me from breathing. I would do whatever it takes to keep inhaling. The unclean spirit does the same. It breaks my concentration so it can inhale."

Then I thought, "Am I hosting an unclean spirit in my mind?"

It was so strange even to consider such a possibility. Yet, the fact was that something—or somebody—in my mind didn't let me stay fully focused. An unclean spirit would be an appropriate name for such a malicious entity.

Once I realized the real depth of my troubles, I increased my meditation time. I solely focused on one task: keeping steady concentration and depriving the unclean spirit of breathing. In addition to late evening meditations, I concentrated for ten minutes every hour at home and in the office.

I began keeping close attention to my thoughts all the time, immediately halting any wandering thoughts. It was the highest point of my spiritual efforts.

One night, I woke up because I felt in my sleep that some force had left my mind. I found myself sitting in the bed. The event was so forceful that it put my body in this position. The next day, I discovered that I could keep my concentration uninterrupted as long as I wanted. With time, I noticed that I became free from episodes of uncontrolled rage and anxiety.

The unclean spirit was gone.

10. The Deviation

A Year Passed

The unclean spirit was gone. After such a success, you might expect that a person would multiply his efforts in a hope to reach a next level. For the next year or so, I did exactly that. I regularly read the Gospel and practiced meditation, enjoying the newly acquired control of my mind. I sought further spiritual advancement.

A year passed, but I remained on the same level. The spiritual advancement didn't happen. Gradually, the routine of life sucked me in. At some point, I lost the focus and began struggling to sustain my spiritual efforts. I lost motivation. The goal had been achieved: my anxiety was gone and life became good.

The Job Offer

One day, my cousin Alex called and invited my wife and me for dinner.

We had a lovely evening. Alex's wife told us about their sailing adventure in the US Virgin Islands. At the end of dinner, Alex offered me the position of director of sales in his start-up business. Recently, he'd he developed the budgeting software and wanted to sale it to regional government s.

I had my doubts. On the one hand, I liked my current structured way of life. I had a decent office job, family time, and my mediations, which I planned to resume. My current pay wasn't astronomical, but it allowed me to provide for my family of four. We already had two children, a five-year-old daughter and a two-year-old son. Being a sales director in a start-up would throw this cozy arrangement out the window. My days would be a mess, extending office hours into late evenings.

On the other hand, if business did well, I would have a chance of earning good money. I also wanted a dynamic and challenging job. Sometimes I felt that I was wasting my life sitting in the office in front of the computer screen all day long.

The Change of Course

I read the Gospel that evening,

> *"But I tell you that anyone who looks at a woman lustfully has already committed adultery with her in his heart. If your right eye causes you to stumble, gouge it out and throw it away. It is better for you to lose one part of your body than for your whole body to be thrown into hell." (Matthew 5:28-29 NIV)*

"It's clear that Jesus doesn't actually want us to gouge an eye out," I thought as I read the verse. "He describes the intensity of the struggle required to free the soul from an unclean spirit."

I felt that something was wrong.

"What is it?" I thought.

Thinking on the spiritual topics used to be the best hour of my day. That evening, I had no interest in thinking.

I felt energy in my heart, and this energy demanded action. I wanted to live a life full of events, desires, and achievements.

I didn't really believe anymore. I mean, if you believe in something, you want to act accordingly to your beliefs. On the contrary, I felt that a strong rejection of Jesus' commands grew in my soul. It wasn't specifically about looking at a woman lustfully. It was about the whole concept of life.

I felt like my spiritual inclinations were lessening my own life.

"Why can't I have a fulfilling, active life? I have only one life, and I am persistently trying to limit my options. Don't do this, don't do that, and don't even look at a woman lustfully. Am I so stupid? I've locked myself in a cell and forbidden myself to venture out. I became afraid of actions. Instead of living, I'm just thinking about life. I am limiting my life. I'm such a miserable, scared fool."

This type of thoughts stormed my mind. The rough wind was filling my sails. The ship headed into wild waters.

The desire to have an action-packed life had always sat deep in my soul. I managed to suppress this urge for a while, but now, it was out in full force and threw me off the track. The carousel of my life started spinning fast.

Next morning, I accepted the position.

Active Life

Ten, maybe twelve years passed.

At my new position, I learned how to establish business contacts, how to convince people, and how to make sales. It turned out, I liked to lead and negotiate. I liked to have busy days when one event followed another. The active life builds your confidence. I liked to be in charge.

For the first five-to-seven years, Alex's business grew well. He hired a few developers to extend the functionality of the product. I started making good money. I bought brand new cars for my wife and myself, made extra mortgage payments, and enjoyed Caribbean vacations three or four times a year.

It was nice to have more money than I needed to get by. For the first time in my family life, I had cash for my own entertainment. On the downside, my working hours were long, I went for business trips frequently, and I abandoned my meditations almost entirely. Hence, different types of thoughts prevailed in my head.

Once the business was established, Alex started talking nonsense. He got an idea that he could live in Florida and manage the business remotely, leaving me to run the operations.

"Well," I said, "in that case I want fifty percent of profit."

Alex found my demand unreasonable; he thought that I should continue working for a salary.

"Such a greedy bastard," we both thought, looking into each other's eyes.

He didn't move to Florida permanently, but instead started building a huge custom house in a wealthy neighborhood. Never-ending construction issues, golfing in the summer, and skiing in the winter kept him out of the office two or three days a week.

I lost my drive to work hard.

Once we paid our mortgage off, I started looking for another job. When I got an offer, I handed to Alex my resignation letter. Secretly, I expected that he would give me a counter-offer with a bigger number. We were sitting in his office.

"Congratulations," he said coldly. "You can leave the office immediately. Talk details with Carol."

I carefully examined his face. He was looking at a screen of his laptop, and then he raised his eyes at me. His face didn't display any shock or disappointment. In a few weeks, I learned why. He was selling the business. My first reaction was anger that he had made the decision to sell behind my back. Then I realized that I didn't care to warn him in advance about my decision to leave, either.

After the sale went through, he sold his new house and moved with his family to Puerto Vallarta, planning to make a living from investments. His dream came true. He also gave me a good severance package, which was very nice of him.

Then the market crashed, he lost his money, moved back to town, and we became close friends again.

11. Profit and Loss

Natural Desire for a Good Life

Twelve years earlier, I had an ambition to become a spiritual man. Then I gave up my beliefs. What had happened? First thing, an excuse came to my mind: I had committed nothing really sinful. All these years, I have been a loving husband and father who tried to do his best at providing for the family.

Yet, the real story was slightly different. I completely abandoned my beliefs for the purpose of making money. During these years, I made only a few weak attempts to return to spiritual thinking. Why did I leave my beliefs with such ease? The simple and natural desire for a good and active life was the reason.

"How could you resist the desire of a good life?" I thought. I felt that such a desire was still sitting deep in my soul.

Finally, I realized that I was at crossroads. I struggled to choose a direction that my life should go in. Remembering my spiritual days, when I tried understanding things, I decided to make it clear for myself where I was standing.

"The problem is I have desires," I thought. "I have desires for simple pleasures like good company, good wine and dining, luxury vacations, exotic trips, sex, and so on."

The problem was that my mind couldn't be devoted to both spiritual aspirations and my desire for pleasures. I needed to choose one of them: whatever was dearer to my heart.

Profit

I sought advice in the Gospel,

> *"For what will it profit a man if he gains the whole world and forfeits his soul? Or what shall a man give in return for his soul?" (Matthew 16:26)*

Profit is financial gain. It is calculated as the difference between the amount earned and the amount spent in buying, operating, or producing something. Jesus uses the concept of profit throughout his teachings. We can find this idea in two of his parables, the Parable of the Talents, Matthew 25:14-28, and the Parable of the Wise Merchant, Matthew 13:45-46.

The question "What will it profit a man?" is a perfect example of Jesus' preaching style. He has something on his mind, but doesn't say exactly what it is. He creates intellectual context and leaves it to us to figure out the answer.

Jesus brings two opposing concepts (profit and soul), blends them together, and makes an intriguing connection. "What will it profit a man?" By asking this question, he tries to find common ground with us. We all agree that it's fitting for an intellectual being to seek beneficial and good things.

Making a financial profit matches our intellectual capacity. We must understand how the specific segment of the market works, come up with our own product or service, and successfully implement it. Only a focused, devoted individual can accomplish such a thing. It seems that the one who gains the whole world has done the right thing. He or she put the mind at work and succeeded to make a profit.

Jesus has a different opinion. To make his point, he brings up the notion of a soul.

Money

The Greek word κερδαίνω (kerdainó), which is translated as "to gain", is an ancient commercial term for exchanging (trading) one item for another. Figuratively, it means to exchange a mediocre item for a better or more expensive and valuable item, i.e., "trading up."[viii]

Money is "a medium that can be exchanged for goods and services and is used as a measure of their values on the market."[ix] The amount of money you possess is also a measure of your wealth. Gaining profit is a challenging task that requires intense efforts. Many people feel that making money is the best use of their time.

From Jesus' point of view, these efforts don't lead to trading up. You would exchange something of great value (the mental force of our soul) for a mediocre thing (material wealth).

Jesus recognizes the human soul as an entity that holds more value than any material wealth. Money has value only because we all agree to accept it as our method of payment. The ability to agree or disagree is a function of the intelligent soul. If the human soul had no ability, money would be worthless.

From this point of view, Jesus is right. Money plays a secondary role in your life, and the intellectual qualities of your soul are the main feature.

Jesus proposes the pursuit of the heavenly kingdom as a worthy use of your mental energy. Allegedly, such efforts will lead to trading up because you would exchange something of great value (the creative force of your soul) for a more exciting thing (a timeless state of being).

Small Gains

A soul outweighs any material possessions because she is the entity that registers the fact of owning. If a soul is gone, nothing is left that could appreciate the feeling of power and wealth. The soul is your true self. Your soul is the greatest wealth you'll ever have.

According to Jesus, the emotions that motivate you to gain power and wealth are the same emotions that corrupt your soul.

Jesus uses an exaggerated comparison—the whole world versus a single soul—to make you think about your own circumstances. A man who conquers the whole world at least has something to brag about. What do you profit when you become dishonest and greedy while pursuing small gains?

It's hard to overcome emotions because they are so embedded in your thinking. You consider them as a part of your personality, but they're not. They're dangerous, deceiving foes. They challenge you every day.

Looking Good at the Final Judgment

If a farmer stops caring for his land, the weeds pollute the soil and choke the plants, preventing them from producing fruits.

If the body's immune system stops recognising viruses as non-self elements, the body gets sick. The viruses trick the cells into reproducing the viruses' DNA instead of the cells' own DNA.

If you don't see negative emotions as a dangerous force, your mind gets corrupted. The virus of emotions fools your mind to produce anxiety, anger, or greed instead of your own thinking. Negative emotions ruin your mood and character. Potentially, they could ruin your life.

Yet, the key issue is that negative emotions make your soul unattractive. You won't look good at the Final Judgment, when God's angels come out to select beautiful souls for eternal life.

Can you blame God's angels? You're attracted to beautiful faces. They're attracted to beautiful souls.

~ If you like this book, please leave a review ~

Acknowledgements

I would like to express my gratitude to everyone who provided support in writing this book; who read, proofread, offered comments, and edits.

Above all, I want to thank my wife for her patience, love and support.

If you would like to support this independent author, please buy his other equally thoughtful and entertaining books:

The Curious Occurrence of Life: *Which Scientific Discovery Proves God?*

Sometimes scientific theories leave the realm of science and become popular beliefs. The theory of evolution is a good example. Often, the theory is used to endorse atheism, and the public assumes that life's evolution is conclusive evidence against God's existence.

In this short book, the author compares Jesus' and Darwin's views on the origin of life. The author discovers that one of the recent major scientific discoveries actually supports Jesus' view rather than Darwin's.

You just need to ask the right question... And you will see that everything is much stranger than you can ever imagine.

Your Awesome Intellect: *How to Reboot the Right Side of Your Mind*

Modern philosophers often see the human inner-self—or consciousness—as an illusion.

In this book, the author seeks a meaningful vision of life. He believes that his mind is real. Unexpectedly, he finds support for his thoughts in the Gospels.

In a nutshell, Jesus rejects a materialistic worldview. He teaches that the creativity of your intellect is a sensational force. Your intellectual talent enables you to think and to grow spiritually. Jesus promises that an ingenious and evolving soul will be invited to enter into a different state of being—the *eternal* state...

Being a skeptic, the author asks, "How does Jesus prove his spectacular teaching?"

Recharge Your Mission: *What Idea Is So Widely Accepted People Believe It's True*

Do you sometimes feel that there should be more to life than what you've been told? Maybe it's because you've never been told the right things.

In this book, the author—a professional computer programmer—questions his beliefs. He distrusts academic scholars and seeks his own answers. As soon as he digs a little deeper, he discovers many bizarre things.

The author learns that secular views are rooted in false assumptions. It changes everything…

If You Feel Lost: *What Important Condition of Your Life You Don't Know*

The recent global tendencies unsettle the author. Seeking a fresh start, he looks into religious ideas hoping to find joy and peace there. He reads the Gospel with an independent mindset. It turns out that the ancient book tells not only the Good News. There is another, rather chilling news also.

This motivates the author to rethink his understanding of life.

Your spirit is a beautiful living being and it can't survive in the darkness of lies. To do well, your spirit needs the light of spiritual knowledge.

Notes

[i] Johnston, Mark (1995). "Self-Deception and the Nature of Mind". *Philosophy of Psychology: Debates on Psychological Explanation*. Cambridge: Blackwell. pp. 63–91.

[ii] Wikipedia contributors, "Lottery scam," *Wikipedia, The Free Encyclopedia*, https://en.wikipedia.org/w/index.php?title=Lottery_scam&oldid=749945101 (accessed March 1, 2017).

[iii] Koonin EV, Senkevich TG, Dolja VV. "The ancient Virus World and evolution of cells", *Biology Direct,* 2006

[iv] Shors, Teri (2008). *Understanding Viruses*. Jones and Bartlett Publishers. ISBN 0-7637-2932-9, p. 54.

[v] Smith A.D. (Ed), *Oxford dictionary of biochemistry and molecular biology*. (1997) Oxford University Press. ISBN 0-19-854768-4;

[vi] Thayer's Greek Lexicon, Electronic Database. Copyright © 2002, 2003, 2006, 2011 by Biblesoft, Inc, http://biblehub.com/thayers/2889.htm (accessed March 1, 2017).

[vii] Richard Feynman (1970). The Feynman Lectures on Physics Vol II. Addison Wesley Longman. ISBN 978-0-201-02115-8.

[viii] HELPS™ Word-studies (2011) by Helps Ministries, Inc. Also available at http://biblehub.com/greek/2770.htm

[ix] TheFreeDictionary © 2016 by Farlex, Inc. Also

available at http://www.thefreedictionary.com

www.ingramcontent.com/pod-product-compliance
Lightning Source LLC
Chambersburg PA
CBHW021143020426
42331CB00005B/880

* 9 7 8 1 9 8 9 6 9 6 2 0 0 *